D1454786

30-MINUTE SOLUTI

How to Make Winning Presentations

30 Action Tips for Getting Your Ideas Across with Clarity and Impact

By
Paul R. Timm, Ph.D.

CAREER PRESS
3 Tice Road
P.O. Box 687
Franklin Lakes, NJ 07417
1-800-CAREER-1
201-848-0310 (NJ and outside U.S.)
FAX: 201-848-1727

30-MINUTE SOLUTIONS SERIES:
HOW TO MAKE WINNING PRESENTATIONS
ISBN 1-56414-326-0, $7.99
Cover design by L & B Desktop Publishing & Printing
Printed in the U.S.A. by Book-mart Press

To order this title by mail, please include price as noted above, $2.50 handling per order, and $1.50 for each book ordered. Send to: Career Press, Inc., 3 Tice Road, P.O. Box 687, Franklin Lakes, NJ 07417.

Or call toll-free 1-800-CAREER-1 (NJ and Canada: 201-848-0310) to order using VISA or MasterCard, or for further information on books from Career Press.

Library of Congress Cataloging-in-Publication Data

Timm, Paul R.
    How to make winning presentations : 30 action tips for getting your ideas across with clarity and impact / by Paul R. Timm.
        p.   cm. -- (The 30-minute training series)
    Originally published: [S.l.] : Jack Wilson & Associates, 1994.
    Includes index.
    ISBN 1-56414-326-0
    1. Business presentations.   I. Title. II. Series.
HF5718.22.T55   1997
658.4'5--dc21   97-7916
                                                                          CIP

Dedication

To my first "speech" teacher, oh so many years ago:

Dr. Charles Petrie at the
State University of New York at Buffalo

Contents

Chapter 1

Make Presentations Work for You

"The most important thing I learned in school was how to communicate."

—Lee Iacocca,
former CEO, Chrysler Corp.

We all make presentations every day

Presentation is the term we use to refer to all kinds of purposeful communication. When we plan, prepare, and create a message to deliver to others, we are making a presentation. These are not speeches, although a speech can be one form of a presentation. Often they are much less formal.

In short, we all spend large portions of our life "making presentations." In fact, we are constantly communicating. We cannot *not* communicate. Everything we say and do, as well as all that we *are*, communicates meaning to others.

The challenge is not to decide *when* to communicate—when to make presentations—but rather how to take control of the process that is going on—communication.

Get the most from your study of presentation skills

The way we communicate has been learned over our entire life. We do what we do because we are comfortable acting that way. We have found our comfort zone—a place in which what we do feels right.

Often our comfort zone limits us too much. In fact, any change and any skill-building requires that we step out of the comfort zone, that we try some new behaviors.

The first time we try anything new can be difficult. But with increased experience, the clumsy becomes smooth, the difficult becomes easier, the scary becomes, well, almost comfortable.

Life is a constant process of experimentation and learning. And because so much of life's successes depend on presenting ideas, doesn't it make sense to build your presentation skills? If you are willing to push out of your comfort zone a bit, you are ready to try on new behaviors.

How to Make Winning Presentations will give you many ideas, but the ideas themselves won't do any good until you try them. Study the Action Tips in this book, apply them, and you'll see a dramatic improvement in your ability to get your ideas across with clarity and impact. After each attempt at something new, look at your results. Think about what went well, what didn't go so well, and how to try it a little differently next time.

✧ Action Tip 1 ✧

Know your attitudes toward making presentations.

Try the following "communicator's self-inventory" to get a clear picture of your attitudes about communicating. Oral communication skills and attitudes improve through evaluation and feedback—from others and from yourself. This self-inventory identifies your starting point. When you've finished this book, retake this quiz and see how much you've grown.

This measurement, like others in this program, will be useful to you only to the degree to which you are totally honest in your answers.

Read each statement and circle yes or no. After answering yes or no, review each answer, and circle the (+) or (-) to indicate how you feel about your answer. A plus means you are satisfied; a minus means you wish you could have answered otherwise. Answer honestly based upon how you actually feel or act, not how you *wish* you would.

Review your self-inventory. For each item where you circled a minus sign (indicating that you don't feel good about your answer), write a goal for personal improvement. Your goal should be specific and clear. For example, if you write a goal for statement 3, you might say, "I will start conversations with one person I don't know each day this week." For statement 15, you might say, "I will learn to listen more carefully." For statement 22 you might say, "I will make a list and learn the pronunciation of one difficult word each day."

Communicator's self-inventory

1. I often have great ideas I'd like to share with other people.
   yes   no   (+)   (-)

2. I enjoy trying to explain my ideas to others.
   yes   no   (+)   (-)

3. I often get the conversation going among my friends and even with people I don't know.
   yes   no   (+)   (-)

4. When I stand up to speak in any group, I get "stage fright."
   yes   no   (+)   (-)

5. Before trying to influence others, I make it a point to be certain that I know what I'm talking about.
   yes   no   (+)   (-)

6. When I disagree with others, the argument often becomes too heated, and afterwards I regret what I've said.
   yes   no   (+)   (-)

7. I usually keep calm and poised, even in discussions where I disagree.
   yes   no   (+)   (-)

8. I am good at persuading others to agree with my views.
   yes   no   (+)   (-)

9. I would have more influence in my job and in social settings if I could better communicate my feelings and ideas.

  yes no   (+)   (-)

10. I regularly clip and save ideas from things I read.

  yes no   (+)   (-)

11. When I know something that could be helpful to others, I like to share this information with them.

  yes no   (+)   (-)

12. In conversations, I enjoy listening even more than I do talking.

  yes no   (+)   (-)

13. While listening to others, I try to identify and organize the main ideas being spoken.

  yes no   (+)   (-)

14. When communicating, I consider feelings and attitudes to be at least as important as facts and ideas.

  yes no   (+)   (-)

15. In comparison to my friends, I think I listen more carefully than they do.

  yes no   (+)   (-)

16. In comparison to my peers, I think that I generally speak more effectively than they do.

  yes no   (+)   (-)

17. I have a good vocabulary.

    yes   no   (+)   (-)

18. My physical delivery (use of hands, posture, expressiveness) is one of my strongest communication skills.

    yes   no   (+)   (-)

19. My voice is pleasant and easy to listen to.

    yes   no   (+)   (-)

20. I am eager to hear helpful criticism from others.

    yes   no   (+)   (-)

21. Improving my communication skills is one of my highest priorities.

    yes   no   (+)   (-)

22. I speak clearly and pronounce words correctly.

    yes   no   (+)   (-)

23. People seem to enjoy what I say; I hold their interest.

    yes   no   (+)   (-)

24. I am good at telling stories or jokes.

    yes   no   (+)   (-)

25. I feel that I am getting better and better in my communication skills.

    yes   no   (+)   (-)

Chapter 2

Overcome Presentation Anxiety

"The human brain is a wonderful organ. It starts working as soon as you are born and doesn't stop until you get up to deliver a speech."

—George Jessel, Vaudeville actor
and comedian

Do you feel that flush of nervousness when asked to introduce yourself to a group or committee? Do you have nightmares about being forced to give a speech in front of a crowd—naked? Have you bottled up a good idea rather than "risk" speaking up in a meeting?

If you answer yes to any of these questions, you are not unusual. We all feel somewhat nervous when all eyes turn to us.

The following Action Tips include proven ways to reduce discomfort, but don't expect it to go away totally. That really isn't even desirable. Anxiety plays an important role in keeping us mentally alert. Yes, nervousness can be our friend.

✧ Action Tip 2 ✧

Build speaking confidence through preparation.

Several steps can be taken to reduce distractions and help you focus on your presentation, thus reducing your fear. The most powerful idea is summed up in one word: *Prepare!*

Nothing reduces anxiety like being well-prepared to the point of being overprepared—totally confident of your grasp of the subject matter.

When preparing, put special emphasis on the opening remarks and the conclusion. If the opener goes well (because you've practiced it over and over), you'll gain confidence for the rest of the presentation.

It may seem awkward at first, but making your presentation into a mirror, videotaping your talk or—best yet—presenting to a practice audience of people who will give you honest feedback will give you lots of good ideas for improvement.

✧ Action Tip 3 ✧

Be idea-conscious, not self-conscious.

Having your specific purpose in mind helps reduce excessive concern for irrelevant details. The workings of our "unconscious success mechanism" enter here. This mechanism is the part of our brain that focuses on the desired goal and allows the unconscious mind to get us there. We are most effective when we don't think of each step of each procedure needed to complete a task but instead focus on the desired result and *allow* our mind to help us get there.

The baseball outfielder going after a high fly ball doesn't consciously think, "I'll take six steps to my left, two steps forward, raise my glove with my left hand and shield my eyes from the sun with my right hand..." Instead he fixes his eyes on the ball and visualizes the desired result of catching it. His unconscious success mechanism handles the details. He doesn't need to think about the little things that might go wrong. He doesn't bother with concerns about tripping over his shoelace, taking the wrong size steps or raising his glove too late. He lets success happen.

The same principle applies in any planned oral communication. Too much concern with mechanics once you've reached the point of doing the presentation can only distract and create anxiety.

The advice speaking coaches give applies nicely to your presentations:

Self-consciousness tends to be self-destructive. If you are overly worried about the way you look, you often overcompensate, and this draws attention which would not ordinarily be centered on you. It's when you are trying to walk nonchalantly that you walk stiffly or affectedly. It is when you are trying to smile naturally (say "cheese") that your smile tends to look artificial. If you are caught up in conversation or telling a story and the conversation of the story causes you to smile, you are usually unaware of the smile itself, and it is at that point that the smile is, and appears, most natural. It's similar when speaking before others. When you are caught up in the message and interested in communicating the ideas to the listeners, you are not usually uncomfortable or noticeably concerned with how you look or how you sound—it's the idea that is at center stage, not the self. Simple remedies: Be listener-centered; be message-centered, not self-centered.[1]

✧ Action Tip 4 ✧

Relax. Your listeners want you to succeed.

Easier said than done, you may say. Sure, but if you are well-prepared and idea-conscious instead of self-conscious,

---

[1] Harold P. Zelco and Frank E. X. Dance, *Business and Professional Speech Communication*, 2nd ed. (Holt, Rhinehart and Winston, 1978), pp. 77-79.

anxiety should not be a problem. You may still feel that flush of nervousness just as you are being introduced or beginning your talk, but it will soon leave because you are prepared.

Such nervousness is perfectly natural and is seldom visible to your listeners. If it is mildly visible, the listener isn't likely to judge you a failure; he is much more likely to empathize. It could be him next!

Remember that your listeners want you to succeed. When people have taken the time to hear what you have to say, they don't want to feel their time has been wasted. Even listeners who strongly disagree with you—hostile listeners—want you to explain yourself clearly if for no other reason than that they can then attempt to shoot down your ideas.

A poor presentation can be just as embarrassing and uncomfortable for the audience as it is for the speaker, sometimes even more so. Just think of times you've seen people do a poor job expressing an idea. What has your re-action been? You probably felt some embarrassment and may have found yourself trying to rephrase their ideas for them. The naive or inexperienced speaker may be unaware of a poor-quality talk, while listeners may be embarrassed for him or her.

No one is out to get you. Just as you want speakers to succeed, your listeners want you to succeed.

✧ Action Tip 5 ✧

Use physical techniques to reduce anxiety.

Although much of what we do to reduce anxiety involves changing our mental attitudes, we can also do some physical things:

1. Take several slow, deep breaths before speaking.

2. Relax your shoulders, neck and any tight muscles.

3. Take a moment to look into your listeners' eyes. Smile.

4. Greet your listeners as they (or you) come into the room.

5. Use your natural, conversational voice. Don't try to sound different or force your ideas with your voice.

6. Dress sharp. Wear the kind of clothing that makes you feel well-dressed and confident. Be sure your dress is appropriate for the occasion. When in doubt, see what others are wearing in similar situations.

7. Practice, practice, practice. Listen to your words and tone of voice from the viewpoint of your listeners.

8. Watch your movements, posture, and appearance. Look for potentially annoying habits (like saying "um" or "okay" or "ya know") and distracting behaviors (such as pacing, jingling keys in your pocket, and twirling a pencil while talking).

✧ **Action Tip 6** ✧

Tune out negative self-talk and perception.

We all talk to ourselves, and much of what we say is negative or limiting. Too often, we use negative self-talk to work ourselves into a dither of anticipated rejection and failure.

We need to realize we have choices concerning what we say to ourselves in stress situations. First, we must recognize that we are in charge of our own self-talk "program"—playing out uninterrupted in our head—that is responsible for creating anxiety. Then we must take steps to change that program so that it works for us rather than against us.

Our perceptions are the way we see the world. Self-talk is the way we comment on these perceptions and relate them to us. Here is a simple example:

As a small child, Rick was mauled by a mean dog. That experience led to a dislike of dogs. Even as an adult, Rick sees dogs as a threat. His self-talk includes statements like, "That mutt looks like he could bite me," or " I hope there are no dogs in this neighborhood." Rick's perception of dogs in general comes from a bad experience with one dog. His self-talk gives voice to his negative thoughts. Eventually, the self-talk programs are replayed enough within Rick's mind that his "dogs-are-bad" belief becomes a fact for him. Truth.

To overcome communication barriers arising from perception and self-talk, we need to listen carefully and objectively. Is what our mind is telling us really truth? Here are some steps to help decide:

Identify your self-talk. As you experience a stressful situation or bad mood, write or tape-record all your self-talk for a period of several minutes. Then analyze what you're saying. Assess your self-talk from several vantage points:

- **Labeling.** Identify the negative self-labels you might be using to tear down yourself. Words like lazy, shy, clumsy, forgetful, loser, sloppy, careless, disorganized or irresponsible may be popping up in your everyday self-talk. You could be using labels like these dozens of times a day, saying things like "I keep fumbling over my words. I sound stupid," or "I should have thought that through before opening my big mouth. I'm such a dunce." Work hard to eliminate these kinds of labels. They do you no good and can really beat up your self-confidence.

- **"Shoulds" and "oughts."** Used frequently, these pesky words create loads of guilt. Instead of "I should have done a better job," say, "I chose to do the job this way for a reason. Perhaps I can do it another way next time." Instead of "I ought to be more organized," say, "I think I'll work at being more organized. It is to my advantage."

- **Gloomy and pessimistic talk.** You may be manufacturing hundreds of negative statements in your mind every day—things like "Nothing ever goes right for me," "It's no use!," "I just can't take it anymore" or "It's going to be another one of those days."

If you find gloom and doom statements in your self-talk, decide to eliminate them. Instead, substitute hopeful statements: "I'm going to look for things that go right today," "I am a survivor. I can take it!" or "I'm going to make this a good day." Take responsibility and practice positive self-talk for yourself.

Past hurts. Does your mind dwell on hurts that occurred weeks, months, or even years ago? Does a new, fresh incident recall other times that you've been hurt by one person or another? If so, you may be using selective self-talk—talk that blames others for wrongs they've caused but does not assign any responsibility to you for events that have occurred.

Blaming talk that constantly reviews past hurts will keep you experiencing pain, discouragement, and often anger. Break the chain by confining your self-talk to the present. Manage the problem by finding ways of releasing and letting go of the pain.

Entrenched programs. If you find you have deeply entrenched habits of self-talk, try a technique known as "thought stoppage." As soon as you're into your automatic self-talk program, break up the thought habits by giving yourself the command to STOP! Then switch your thoughts to a pleasant or neutral subject. Like the clipped, compelling command of a drill sergeant, your command needs to be strong enough to startle your thought process.

✧ Action Tip 7 ✧

Build your personal credibility.

Aristotle wrote about communication in *The Rhetoric*. There he explained that there are three types of arguments or forms of persuasion one may use to convince people:

1. Logical appeals (logos).

2. Emotional appeals (pathos).

3. Ethical appeals (ethos).

Ethos (ethical appeals), according to tradition, is the most important of the three classical concepts. In regard to ethos, Aristotle said:

There are three things which inspire confidence in the communicator's own character—the three, namely, that induce us to believe a thing apart from any proof of it: good sense, good moral character and good will... There is no proof so effective as that of the character.

The term ethos is what we now call speaker *credibility.* Credibility is faith placed in you by others who perceive you as being intelligent, as having high standards, as being trustworthy, and so forth. It is cumulative and ongoing. What you say or do today will have a bearing on how others view your credibility tomorrow.

A massive amount of research on credibility has sought to further define what factors determine how others see our credibility. The findings suggest four important factors of credibility:

1. **Expertise.** The degree to which you are informed about a particular topic affects your credibility. Generally, someone with high credibility has had training and/or experience *relevant to the topic* and is capable of displaying this competence. Citing other recognized experts on the subject will help convey such expertise.

2. **Trustworthiness.** Credibility goes up when a communicator appears to be sincere and unbiased. You can create that impression by using facts and careful reasoning and by avoiding language that conveys undue emotionalism.

   Another technique that creates trust is to recognize and present opposing points of view. Such action shows that you are unbiased and not given to making hasty judgments.

Finally, if you have *no secret motive*, such as personal gain, to be achieved from your talk, your credibility grows. The salesman for TV advertising is likely to be less credible in an open discussion of the advantages of various ad media than, say, an individual who handles all types of advertising programs.

3. **Composure.** Another factor affecting credibility is the degree of poise and confidence a communicator displays. The nonverbal factors such as appearance, posture, mannerisms, and facial expressions combine to create an impression for an audience. The speaker who is overly nervous, disorganized, or disheveled has low credibility. Most people prefer someone who looks his or her best and is positive, confident, spontaneous, and humble.

4. **Dynamism.** Credibility is also influenced by your personal dynamism: the tendency to be outgoing, friendly, and articulate. A shy, apprehensive person often appears less credible that his or her more extroverted counterpart. However, we suggest moderation; the loudmouthed, totally uninhibited character may be dynamic but not very credible.

Of these dimensions of credibility, trustworthiness has repeatedly been shown to be the most important.

✧ Action Tip 8 ✧

Be realistic about your intent.

When specifying the topic of your presentation, you should ask yourself another vital question: *"What can I reasonably expect to accomplish from this presentation?"* Put another way, *"What, specifically, do I want from my listeners? How do I want them to respond?"*

Often your intent will be for the listener to learn or do something. Sometimes you may simply want to bring them up-to-date or perhaps entertain them. The clearer your understanding of exactly what you are attempting, the greater your likelihood of success and reduced anxiety. If a speaker's intent is unclear, unrealistic, or unproductive, that speaker is wasting the audience's time. Communicate for specific desired response.

When specifying your intent, be realistic. Even the best communicators do not always get all the listeners to respond as they would wish. Your listeners have minds of their own that sometimes resist what you are saying to them. They may view the topic in another light or simply won't agree with your proposal, no matter how clearly you express yourself. Every good salesperson knows that some people simply will not buy from you no matter what you say or do!

As a general rule, it is easier to change people's knowledge than it is to change their attitudes or behaviors. So, if your presentation is aimed at getting your listeners to do something they wouldn't normally do, your probability of total success is likely to be less than if your intent was simply to inform.

Examples of realistically stated intentions may be:

- I hope to get one sale for each 10 people in the audience.

- I intend to get the boss to agree that we need a budget increase (even if she doesn't go for the full amount I have in mind).

- I expect that the listeners will understand better how to interpret their monthly results printout accurately, thus reducing (but not eliminating) calls to the data processing supervisors.

✧ Action Tip 9 ✧

Remember that you and your listeners need each other.

By coming to your presentation or inviting you to talk, listeners are expressing a need for information, friendship, help, approval, or clarification, maybe even inspiration. They hope that something you say will improve their lives—that you'll share something worthwhile with them.

You as a presenter have needs, too. Probably the strongest need is for approval. Only your listeners can give you this, but it can be shown in many forms, from a simple vote (a raising of hands), to a signature on a document (a sales agreement), to an outburst of applause or a hearty thank-you. Without some indication of approval, response, endorsement, confirmation—*something!*—a presenter is lost at sea, adrift, seeking a signal. This can be tough on the ego. (*No* response is, in many ways, worse than outright rejection.)

✧ Action Tip 10 ✧

Create a conversation circle with your listeners.

Good communication is circular. A message is sent, received, and responded to. Effective communicators always look for feedback and let their listeners know they want them to participate in the communication process.

When communication becomes a circle, we create a close sympathetic relationship based on agreement and harmony. In short, we get to like each other.

A conversation circle emerges when you get your listeners involved. Plan for listener participation in your presentation. A presentation should almost never be delivered in an "I talk, you listen" format. Listener involvement is not only desirable but necessary.

People don't like to be talked *at*; they want to be talked *with*. Even in large group presentations, the most successful communicators create the feeling that they are conversing with each audience member.

People like to participate. The more you can get the listener into the act—doing something with you, mentally or physically—the more interesting you'll be to your listeners.

Strive to manage a learning process, not force-feed information. Just because you're the *speaker* doesn't mean you should do all the talking!

Most presenters err on the side of too little participation rather than too much. The audiences love it; they enjoy it; they will never protest against too much talking or action on their part, but they will regret too little. One often sees speaker evaluation sheets with the comment "not enough group participation; too much monologue." One never sees the comment "too much group participation."

Besides your audience liking participation, it also helps you as the presenter. A quick way to reduce anxiety is to get people involved in your presentation. You'll be more comfortable and so will the listeners.

Allow me to repeat for emphasis: *The most important ingredient to an effective presentation is listener participation.* In some cases, this participation may only be a mental activity. But often—far more often than many communicators realize—there are many opportunities for listener involvement that are both physical and mental. From your own experiences, you have undoubtedly noticed that classes or meetings where you can get involved are simply more enjoyable—and more rewarding.

Give listeners opportunities for involvement, and you'll feel more comfortable and get your ideas across much better. Some simple ways to do this:

1. Let them know that it's okay to ask questions—in fact, encourage it.

2. When they do ask questions, "reward" them by answering the question and thanking them for asking.

3. Look for nonverbal feedback. By observing their body posture, eyes and facial expressions, you can decide if they're getting the message. If you aren't sure they are, ask them.

4. Test for understanding. Ask them to explain in their own words what you've said or how they plan to apply your ideas.

5. Never belittle or embarrass listeners. If they ask a question, they need your answer. Even if the question has already been covered, patiently answer again.

Chapter 3

Avoid the Pitfalls

"The saddest words that clog my head,

Begin like this: 'I should'a said.' "

—Gerald Barzan, poet

Let's talk about two pitfalls that can almost guarantee a poor presentation. Being aware of these can help overcome them:

1. Ineffective use of language.

2. Lack of openness to feedback.

✧ Action Tip 11 ✧

Avoid ineffective use of language.

Despite the fact that the purpose of language is to communicate, our ineffective use of language often produces the opposite result: confusion and misunderstanding.

In the English language, we have approximately 600,000 standard words available for use. We might add to that another 100,000 technical terms, acronyms, jargon, or slang expressions. However, the average adult uses only about 2,000 words on a regular basis. The dilemma, of course, is when we consider the meager store of commonly used words that are used to communicate an unlimited number of different ideas.

A common misconception is that use of multi-syllable words makes us come across as more intelligent. Not so. The best communicators learn to convey even complex ideas with simple, conversational words. Don't use a three- or four-syllable word when a one- or two-syllable one will do the job. Strive to make your presentations sound like one friend speaking to another in a fairly informal situation.

The dilemma of language is further complicated when we realize that much of what we communicate to others is in the form of nonverbal "languages"—ideas communicated without words. As much as 80 percent of the meaning received comes from nonverbal cues. Such things as personal appearance and dress, facial expressions, gestures, message timing, use of space, and many other factors contribute to or detract from the sharing of meaning.

✧ **Action Tip 12** ✧

Be open to feedback.

One of the most critical ingredients in boosting communication skills is to be receptive to feedback—even from your critics. This, of course, can be painful. But it can also be exceptionally valuable.

We never really know how we are coming across to others unless we seek feedback. Ineffective communicators prefer to be ostriches. They bury their heads and tune out all negative comments. In doing so, they never learn what they need to know to improve. But, of course, the ostrich always leaves one end exposed.

For most people, giving criticism (even in a constructive way) is risky. When people first offer such feedback, they watch closely to gauge others' responses. The reaction they receive will usually determine whether they will offer feedback again. This means that you have an opportunity to avoid turning off future feedback that could be valuable to you.

Some tips for encouraging feedback

1. Don't be defensive. Listen—don't explain or justify. Learn to withhold your response. The time to explain or justify your actions is not during the criticism, even if you feel the criticism is unwarranted or stems from a misunderstanding. Listen now, explain later. Your defensiveness stifles feedback. It tells others you are more interested in justifying yourself than in understanding what is being said.

2. Ask for specifics. This is a good opportunity to obtain more information. Honest questions will support and encourage continued feedback. For example, say, "That's very helpful. Tell me more. Is there anything else I should know about that?"

3. Express an honest reaction. You certainly have a right to express your feelings about the feedback received. You may well say, "I'm a little surprised you said that, but you may have a point" or "I'm not sure what to say. I never even thought of that, but I will from now on."

4. Thank those providing feedback, and plan for the future. Let people know that you realize how risky giving feedback can be, and express your appreciation for their efforts. This might also be a good time to plan for future feedback sessions. These will be less disturbing and more productive than the first one because you have demonstrated that you are receptive.

You should realize that few people are completely comfortable with following this advice, not because they wouldn't benefit from these four actions, but because it takes a lot of courage to seek out and really hear feedback—especially criticism.

But the successful communicator is willing to do what the unsuccessful communicator is not. Getting feedback is a classic example of such an action.

Chapter 4

Discover Your Listeners

....

"Better say nothing than not to the purpose. And to speak pertinently, consider both what is fit, and what is fit to speak."

—William Penn, American philosopher, statesman

✧ Action Tip 13 ✧

Understand your listeners' level of understanding.

Story time: Dr. Herb Gilruth is a psychology professor at State University. His niece Sarah teaches third grade at Washington Elementary. As a young, progressive teacher, Sarah thought it would be interesting if Uncle Herb would talk to her class of 8-year-olds about psychology.

Dr. Gilruth responded to her invitation and prepared a half-hour presentation on psychology basics. "Kids," he began, "I'm going to talk with you about psychology, the study of mental processes that have an impact on your everyday life in myriad ways, ranging from your self-concept to your socialization skills. I'll illustrate my main points by citing empirical research that I'm sure you'll find interesting."

How's he doing so far?

After several more minutes of "explanations of the parameters of clinical, abnormal, and social psychology phenomena," the kids started to squirm. But he droned on, oblivious to the fact that no communication was taking place. Sure, he was talking, but no information was being shared. Why not?

The problem here was that the presenter was hopelessly out of touch with his listeners. He normally spoke to college students and was completely unaware (or insensitive to) his young audience. He failed to connect with his listeners—to understand their level of understanding.

Listener analysis means making guesses based on as much information as we can reasonably gather. From these guesses we can determine how best to construct our message for maximum impact.

More to the point, when we bring a message to someone, we picture—we anticipate—how that person is likely to react.

Predicting listener responses is a natural activity for people. But how do you learn to predict accurately? The best approach is to empathize, to constantly put yourself into your listeners' shoes. In so doing, you try to:

1. Recall how you have responded when you received a message that was inappropriate to your level of understanding.

2. Understand the actions, thought, values, and emotions of your listeners, or other people who are similar to your listeners.

In Dr. Gilruth's case, he would have done a lot better to eliminate the multi-syllable words and highly academic terms from his presentation and speak in language an 8-year-old would be familiar with.

✧ Action Tip 14 ✧

Anticipate what your listeners want to know.

You've been asked to give an oral briefing on a rather broad topic, say "technology developments in the modern office." Obviously you can't say everything there is to say about such a topic. So you choose some facts from the mass of available information you think will be useful and interesting. Hopefully, you didn't select those solely on the basis of your interests; you attempted to anticipate your listeners' needs, too.

First, make knowledgeable guesses about listener interests and information needs. These guesses are based on what you know about the listeners or others like them. For our example, say that in earlier presentations you've done, you noticed that people really seemed to perk up when you talked about networking. Thus, as you prepare your presentation for a group of employees, you'll want to focus on technology that facilitates networking. In your conversations with managers, they've expressed a need for faster computers. You'll then want to report on the latest innovations you've witnessed at the "office of the future" trade show you recently attended.

Second, you need to have a good idea how much they already know about the subject. Your listeners will leave you faster than a cheetah leaves a salad bar if you tell them what they already know. They'll feel you are talking down to them or, worse, insulting their intelligence.

On the other hand, it is just as bad to talk about complex information to people who don't yet know the basics. Listeners who are, for example, new to computer technology need to be brought up to date in exactly what small computing systems can do before they're likely to get very excited about purchasing one.

Third, you must *find out how much detail they want or need to know about the topic.* Giving detailed information to people who just want an overview of the material may annoy or bore them. When a listener needs to know what time it is, don't tell him how to build a watch!

When speaking to people within our own organization, we have a distinct advantage over the public speaker in such analysis. To get clear answers to these questions, we can often simply go to the people we will be speaking to and ask them! We can also draw from day-to-day interaction with them at work to get important clues about their needs.

✦ Action Tip 15 ✦

Assess what your listeners expect.

Expectations are often self-fulfilling. People hear what they expect to hear, even if they have to distort the speaker's real message to make it fit what they anticipated.

When your message coincides with what the listener expects, your success is enhanced, unless your listener makes. an "I've heard this all before" assumption. In such cases, details of your message may be lost because your listener feels he or she already knows what you are saying.

If your message presents a point of view very different from what your audience expects from you, it pays to clarify early in the talk the fact that this may not be the message they anticipated.

Organizational position, personality, past behavior, appearance, age, sex, ethnic origin, race, and countless other factors provide clues that we translate into expectations. The leader interested in getting across ideas that vary from these expectations may need to shock his audience into a recognition that the unexpected is being presented. The sales rep may open her pitch with sincere statements: "I'm not here to sell you anything today. In fact, I won't even accept an order from you." This is likely to cause the purchasing agent to readjust his expectations and prepare for an unusual type of presentation. Similarly, the systems analyst who announces that he's "not here to talk about technology" may spark curiosity as well as adjust listener expectations.

It pays to ask yourself: *"What does my audience expect from me?"* If your topic is consistent with what they're likely to anticipate, use this to strengthen your message. If your topic is different, be sure to help them readjust their expectations lest they mentally distort your message and miss the point entirely.

✧ Action Tip 16 ✧

Adjust to your audience throughout the presentation.

The effective communicator makes listener analysis an ongoing process before, during, and after the presentation. The sensitive speaker will get a great deal of information from his or her listeners as the presentation is given.

Often this information is nonverbal—such things as attentiveness, facial expressions, a general sense of restlessness, excitement, passiveness, or apathy. As you labor through the lengthy history of your organization, you may notice the room full of prospective members appears anxious, several are tapping their feet, fidgeting in their chairs or looking at their watches. Take this as a cue to jump ahead to some of the group's exciting activities before your audience starts getting up and walking out the door. Perhaps you notice, as you endorse a controversial zoning issue to a homeowner's association, that heads are shaking, arms are folding, and postures are stiffening. You can be sure that your audience disagrees with you and it's time to present some pretty compelling evidence to support your view—or get out of town fast!

Eye contact—or lack of it, body language, even the level of chair-scooting, paper shuffling, and other room noises convey whether you are coming across effectively. The challenge, of course, is to *adapt and adjust to this feedback* so that you hold your audience's interest. As we will discuss later in this book, such things as physical movements, gestures, and voice changes can do a great deal to animate your presentation.

Build flexibility into any presentation. We can never predict exactly the reactions of our listeners, so be prepared to take a different tack if the feedback you get tells you the listeners need a change.

Chapter 5

Plan Your Approach

··

"Engage brain before putting mouth in motion."

—Common wisdom

✧ Action Tip 17 ✧

Build your presentation around your listeners' questions.

How you present ideas should be determined by the underlying questions—the need for clarification—of your listeners.

Before preparing an oral presentation, you would do well to anticipate as many listener questions as possible. And don't just ask the obvious ones; dig a little to anticipate what else might be on their minds.

The purposes of presentations may be classified into three primary categories (although overlapping and multiple-purpose presentations are not uncommon):

1. Presentations that persuade.

2. Presentations that instruct or explain.

3. Presentations that report progress.

1. Persuasive presentation

A *persuasive presentation* requires you to do three things: convince your listeners of your point of view, get them to agree with that point of view and get them to act on what they have agreed to. The last requirement is especially important because the success of your presentation can be measured by the amount of such actions. Persuasion calls for action.

2. Informative talk

The second class of presentations is the *informative talk*. This class can be further broken down into instructional or explanatory presentation. Instructional presentations offer specific techniques for doing something, while explanatory talks provide listeners with some new knowledge or understanding. The distinction between these is rather subtle but should be kept in mind when defining a specific purpose. Both involve information-giving as their key function. Instruction implies a more "nuts and bolts" orientation, while explanation goes a bit more into the philosophy or background of a policy, procedure, or proposal.

Instructional communication situations invite "testing" your listeners for knowledge gained, either through an oral question-answer session, via a written quiz, or by asking your listeners to perform or demonstrate what they have learned to do. You objective is skill development.

Explanatory presentations usually give a general overall picture of a concept, program, or product rather than specific techniques for doing something. Your objective is listener understanding.

3. Progress reports

Progress reports are presented to keep your listeners posted on the various stages of a long-term project or goal they are already aware of. Often, progress reports are presented at regular intervals, such as monthly or weekly, until the project is completed.

Early identification of the type of speaking you'll be doing should help you to clarify your purpose and your idea organization strategy.

You can clarify your topic by giving it a working title— a statement of your theme. This title should be specific yet need not sound like a newspaper headline. Indeed, a longer, more descriptive title is often better. Instead of talking about "plant safety," we might deal with "reducing accidents in the welding shop." "Billing order accuracy" might become "reducing errors created by data input clerks." Work to use clear, concrete terms, not vague generalities.

In many situations, of course, your title will never be known to your listeners; we seldom announce it except in more formal speaking situations. The title does, however, serve to:

1. Specify and limit the scope of your topic.

2. Remind you to relate what you will say to listeners' benefits.

3. Identify your topic on the agenda of a meeting (where appropriate).

4. Provide a name for your note-gathering file.

✧ Action Tip 18 ✧

Make use of all materials available to you.

Three categories of materials will affect your success: the physical environment, audio/visual support, and your notes and references.

1. Environment

First the *environment* in which you speak should be maximized. Make it conducive to your presentation format and comfortable for your listeners. Check the layout of the room, the furniture, the lighting, the temperature and the sound system before you use the facility. If something isn't functioning properly or needs changing, you can correct it and avoid any last-minute delays or surprises that can rattle your self-confidence.

Sometimes, of course, you have little control over the place where you'll give your pitch. If, for example, you are visiting someone else's office, it may be awkward to re-arrange the furniture. But even here, there are some things you can do: If you find yourself talking over a desk that seems like an imposing barrier, lure your listeners around to your side with visual aids, a hands-on demonstration, or some other ploy. Or ask if you could come around to his or her side so that you can share your important information.

In a conference room or small group setting, get up and move around or even ask listeners to move their chairs around so they can better see your information, which is important to them.

2. Audio-visuals

Develop *audio-visuals* that simplify or reinforce the ideas presented orally. Charts, tables, graphs, handouts, sample equipment, videos, slides, overhead transparencies and the like should be gathered and used as appropriate. We'll look at this in greater detail in Chapter 9 (Action Tip 32). For now, it is important to consider your presentation situation and what types of visuals you may need to use.

3. Notes and references

A third class of material is less tangible, but obviously very important: your information, your *notes and references*. In every speaking situation, some research is needed. The quality of your ideas and information constitute the most important materials of all. Good data does not speak for itself; raw information must be organized into digestible and useful form. Think about the format of your notes. As a general rule, the more concise they are, the better. Having too much information will cause you to *read* rather than present.

✦ **Action Tip 19** ✦

Plan to use frequent summaries.

Summaries tie together main points and help the listener organize and digest the ideas presented. Because most people are rather poor listeners—we forget things shortly after they are said—use summaries liberally. After making two or three points, restate those points (perhaps in a slightly different way) to help cement them into your listeners' minds.

Repetition is an important learning device. The key to speaking success was once summed up this way:

"I tell them what I'm going to tell them; then I tell them what I told them I was going to tell them; and then I tell them what I have told them."

Preview the message, present the message and summarize the message.

Remember, summaries are not just for the end of the talk. Use summaries as often as needed to recap ideas presented to that point in your presentation.

✧ Action Tip 20 ✧

Plan to use a check-up to test for success.

When planning how you will check up on your listeners' retention, use your creativity. The purposes of a check-up are to:

1. Find out what your listener has learned so far.

2. Get feedback on how you can improve your presentation.

You might wonder how you can test an audience for understanding. After all, most of your presentations aren't like school classes where the teacher can use a pop quiz. But let's consider another view: If your topic is important enough to present in the first place, it's certainly important enough to check for understanding.

Here are some techniques for checking up that I've found useful:

• Ask listeners questions and encourage participation by responding positively to their answers. Relate their responses to points you've made in your presentation. Use open-ended questions, not the standard, "Are there any questions?" (It's too easy for them to say no.) Instead ask, "What questions do you have about...?"—a question that says that you expect them to have some.

- Better yet, ask questions such as, "How do you think this idea would work in your area, Tom?" Or "How could you implement something like this, Marsha?"

- When people do respond to your check-up questions, *be sure to "reward" them for responding.* Comments like "I agree" or "good point" go a long way toward encouraging further responses. Even if a comment doesn't make much sense to you, at least thank the person for his or her thoughts. The worst thing we can do is let a person's comment just hang there in a silent vacuum. This will surely kill off future participation.

- Study the nonverbal responses of your listeners while you are presenting. If you see looks of uncertainty or nods that indicate agreement, use these signs as springboards for your questions. Be careful to avoid questions that may embarrass. If a listener looks lost, say, "Carol, I get the feeling I'm not explaining this very well. Can I clear it up for you?" If a listener nods agreement, you might say, "Fred, you look like you've had a similar experience?" Then give him time to describe his experience.

- If an audience has been asked to learn the parts that make up something, you can check up by holding up a chart and asking them to name the components.

- Invite audience participation in reviewing what was learned by asking someone to demonstrate or summarize what you've said.

✧ Action Tip 21 ✧

Give your listeners an assignment.

Go a step beyond check-up, and assign your listeners a little *homework!* It can easily be done, and most people won't fight it. The effective assignment will give the audience something to think about after they have left your presentation. And that, of course, is the reason for its use.

To be effective, show them how they can benefit from continued application of your ideas. Here are some assignments you might give listeners:

- Ask them to review their notes and/or report their progress to someone else within 24 or 48 hours. This will motivate them to rethink the message.

- Ask them to set up their own test by trying out your ideas. Show an interest in hearing how the results turn out. Encourage them to let you know.

- Ask them to look for situations each day that illustrate what you've been saying.

- Recommend other sources where they can get more information about the topic, such as articles, books or movies. Encourage them to send you clippings.

- Extend a challenge to try something new for a short period of time so that they can experience its benefits.

✧ Action Tip 22 ✧

Give listeners something to take home.

Plan to give some tangible reminder the listener can take away to remind him or her of your message. The reason is similar to that for the assignment step. Take-home items can keep teaching after you're gone.

These items can be of many forms, including samples, outlines, charts, letters, brochures, badges, coffee mugs, hats, photos, and so on. The take-home may produce the added benefit of advertising to others who have not heard your presentation. When an office visitor asks about the coffee mug or baseball hat, your listener has an opportunity to repeat your message.

Keep take-home items simple and appropriate to the topic. Call attention to your take-home items during the presentation and explain them in terms of what good they'll do for your audience. Do not, however, pass out reading material while you are speaking or you may lose your listener's attention. We can't read and listen at the same time.

Chapter 6

State and Build On Key Ideas

"The ill-prepared communicator 'discloses the workings of a mind to which incoherence lends an illusion of profundity.'"

—T. DeVere White, philosopher

✧ Action Tip 23 ✧

Be clear about your central theme and key ideas.

The central theme is a summary statement of what you intend to prove or demonstrate; it answers the underlying questions that were the reason for your presentation. A statement of central theme should:

1. Link the subject to your purpose and your audience.

2. State what you are going to talk about.

3. Express the idea in simple, precise words.

The central theme determines the shape of the whole presentation. Take time to word your theme carefully, concisely, yet completely. Here are some examples of central themes:

- A plant safety training class should be given to all first-level supervisors.

- We should try a mail-order sales approach for our new line of coaxial coordinators.

- My department budget must be increased by at least 5 percent to meet current work load.

- Each employee should understand pension program eligibility and how benefit amounts can be calculated.

- The new sales compensation plan provides greater earning opportunities than ever if sales representatives focus on high-profit items.

- The new computer network software is a smart buy for this company.

Once the central theme is specified, it becomes easier to distinguish key ideas that become the "bones" of your presentation. Each "bone" must clearly support the central theme.

What are my key ideas?

Key ideas are the major thoughts, facts, or concepts that you want the audience to remember from your presentation. For example, let's build on the last central theme example cited above. Say that you have been asked to check out network software at a trade show. You are impressed and think your company should buy such a package. Based on audience analysis, you know your listeners are skeptical about purchasing this software because it costs more than competing equipment. You decide that the main points you want the audience to know are these:

1. The software is 20 percent faster than other products on the market. It's more efficient.

2. The manufacturer has an outstanding reputation for customer support.

3. The manufacturer has promised to train our people at our business location, spending as much time as it takes to be sure everyone knows how to use all features.

4. The company has offered to provide the next upgrade without extra charge.

These are your key selling points. The rest of your talk will build on these ideas. It's important to get these key ideas down on paper so you don't get sidetracked when developing the rest of the presentation.

Here are some points to remember as you list the key ideas for your presentation:

1. State key ideas as if they were conclusions to be drawn at the end of your presentation, preferably in complete sentences.

2. Be sure key ideas relate clearly to your overall main purpose, such as getting agreement, convincing, or generating the desired action.

3. State your ideas in specific terms so that they are thought-provoking.

4. Use only a few key ideas. People have difficulty following more than four points. Two or three would be better.

Once the bones of the presentation are provided via the key ideas, we can begin to fatten up the structure, building on these main points. Key ideas alone rarely convince an audience to accept or agree with your proposal. You must support them: clarify, prove, or elaborate on the key ideas.

✧ **Action Tip 24** ✧

Anticipate listeners' questions.

For each key idea, ask yourself the kinds of questions your listeners might ask. Then devise answers for these questions. In the chart on page 55 are some examples of key ideas and the potential questions listeners may ask:

How much support is needed? That depends on the listeners' attitudes toward what you will say. Attitudes can be:

- Accepting (they tend to agree with you).

- Skeptical (they're not sure).

- Opposed (they object or see things differently).

Key idea	Potential questions
The company should offer marriage and family counseling to employees at no cost.	Is this an appropriate benefit for employees? Or, How could this affect company results?
Sales on product X rose an astonishing 80 percent in the past month.	What accounted for the sharp increase?
[in a job interview] I earned the rank of Eagle Scout at age 15.	How does this accomplishment relate to your potential in this company?
Customers are different today than they were 10 years ago.	How do they differ?

Make your best guess about attitudes toward each key idea. The *skeptical* or *opposed* listener will need more supporting data for the idea.

✧ Action Tip 25 ✧

Use a variety of support for key ideas.

The most interesting speakers use a variety of types of support for their key ideas:

Details or explanations of each key idea simply restate or explain in different words what the key idea asserts. This support may be prefaced by such remarks as "Let me explain why I've said that," or "Another way to say this might be...". From my experience, people rely too heavily on this type of support when other, more interesting ways could be used. Try, instead, to use some other techniques, such as the following:

Comparisons or analogies often provide excellent support. An apt analogy can communicate ideas far more clearly and interestingly than a mere explanation can. Often analogies are short stories with an appropriate lesson.

Examples, especially those from your personal experience, are good sources of support for key ideas; they also give you credibility by showing your experience.

Definitions are sometimes useful to support key ideas by clarifying specialized terms your listeners may not know. Put these into your own words rather than read from a dictionary—and be careful not to talk down to your audience. You might say something like "Many of you are familiar with semiconductor technology, but let me review quickly what I mean for those who aren't."

Often a humorous definition can be effective at holding attention and making a point. "Diplomacy has been defined as the art of letting someone else have your way" is catchy and could well support a key idea. Comedian George Gobel once defined a salesman as "a guy with a smile on his face, a shine on his shoes, and a lousy territory." Salespeople who are known to complain about their territory will laugh at that.

Taking a moment to define a term that may be unfamiliar ensures that your audience can stay with you. Often listeners will not risk embarrassment by asking you to define a term; you should take the initiative to clarify.

Statistics provide another means of supporting a key idea. Mark Twain's oft-quoted line, "There are liars and there are damn liars; and then there are statistics" points out a potential problem. You no doubt know ways in which statistics can be used to distort information, but any form of "lying with statistics" is a poor choice and will eventually cause a gap in your credibility. Be comfortable with the statistics and their implications before you use them. If you decide to use statistics, these guidelines will help you use them more effectively:

1. Round off large numbers so they are more easily grasped.

2. Interpret the numbers so they are meaningful to the listeners. Percentages can be understood by most people.

3. Use statistics sparingly. Anything used to excess becomes commonplace or boring.

4. Be sure to compare "apples to apples." I once heard a speaker express relief that our unemployment rate was only 6 or 7 percent. "In Israel," she exclaimed, "one person in 18 is unemployed!" That, of course, is virtually the same percentage.

The formal quotation can be effective if we choose to quote an authority who is:

1. Recognized as an expert by your listeners.

2. In a position to know about the specific point you are trying to support.

3. In general agreement with other authorities on the subject.

4. Free from prejudice that would distort his or her view.

The person you quote doesn't have to be a national or international figure. It may be someone in your own organization who has had a lot of training or experience and whose ideas and name would be recognized and valued by your listeners.

Audio-visual supports are becoming more important because your listeners have grown up in a "television age" and are conditioned to visual as well as spoken messages. Visuals can be used in conjunction with any kind of support to enhance your presentation. (See Chapter 9.)

Support from your listeners is one other technique that should be used whenever possible. Here, you get the listeners to participate in making your case by having them provide information. Let's say, for example, that your talk is stressing the need for additional security in a retail store, and your audience includes several store managers. Instead of quoting statistics, you might ask the store managers specific questions—preferably ones they're likely to know the answers to! "Margaret, how much has your store lost to shoplifters this year?" or "How do these losses compare to last year?" Be sure that you have information in case Margaret can't recall off hand. And be careful not to embarrass her if she doesn't know.

✧ Action Tip 26 ✧

Arrange your ideas for clarity and impact.

Let me introduce you to my friends, Bif and Bill: Remember their names, and you are on your way to better organization already.

BIF = **B**ig **I**dea **F**irst

BILL = **B**ig **I**dea a **L**ittle **L**ater

But what is this thing called the "big idea"? It is simply *what you want your listener to do or think* when you have finished your presentation.

BIF and BILL are two patterns of organization. When your listener is not likely to resist or be opposed to your big idea, put it first—right up front in your presentation. Use BIF for good news and routine or neutral messages, and issues that your listeners are unlikely to get too emotional about.

Use BILL when your listener may have some emotional resistance to your ideas, such as when conveying bad news or attempting to persuade your audience to a different viewpoint.

The key element in deciding if BIF or BILL works better is the listener's emotional involvement. Two types of emotion are particularly important: disappointment (such as when bad news is received), and reluctance (such as when someone is trying to sell or persuade the listener).

When conveying bad news, it usually helps reduce the pain by building up to the big idea *after* explaining reasoning. For example, if a listener is being refused a promotion he applied for, a BILL approach would explain the decision criteria used to promote someone else before just saying, "You didn't get the job." (Some people, however, prefer to hear it straight, and you'll need to be sensitive to that desire.)

Likewise, when selling something—a process that requires the listener to do something he or she might not otherwise do—a BILL approach makes sense. Present the reasons, the features, the benefits of the product you are selling before getting to the big idea, which is, "I want you to buy this." Starting out the presentation with "I want to sell you some insurance," or the like, probably will to turn off your listener.

Chapter 7

Build Beginnings, Bridges, and Endings

"A speech is like a love affair. Any fool can start it, but to end it requires considerable skill."

—Lord Mancroft,
British statesman

The most critical points in a presentation are the beginning and the ending. Great communicators make the most of these and use transitions to bridge these together so that listeners follow the flow of remarks.

✧ Action Tip 27 ✧

Use beginnings to create expectations and introduce your message.

The introduction is not just an attachment we tack on to the beginning of a talk. It serves important purposes. When successful it should:

1. Get the listeners' attention.
2. Introduce the listeners to the theme of the presentation (thus creating expectations).
3. Establish credibility.

In addition to these, an introduction may also:

1. Disclose the central theme.
2. Limit the scope of the presentation.
3. Directly state a conclusion, especially using a BIF approach.

Here is an example of a speaker's opening remarks that create appropriate expectations by telling exactly what will be covered, using a BIF pattern of arrangement:

"Folks, I've been asked to explain the new sales commission program, and I think you're going to like it. You can make a lot more money than you now do if you'll do one simple thing: sell the machines that make the company the best profits. Here's the deal..."

Here is an example of creating expectations that will lead into a BILL approach message:

"The ideas I'm going to discuss with you today are not going to be popular. But right now I need to be more concerned with the success of our project than with my personal popularity..."

The above examples show how expectations can be created—one part of the introduction process. But as opening remarks, they can be improved upon by using some proven techniques for introducing a presentation.

Statement of purpose

At times a simple statement of what you'll be covering is an adequate opening remark—but not often! We too often hear such lukewarm statements as "Jack asked me to say a few words about..." or "I'm going to cover the policy change dealing with...".

Of all the readily available introductory techniques, this is the weakest. Its main drawback is that, unless the topic is of some vital interest to your listeners (perhaps the examples above would be such cases), you aren't offering them a good reason to listen by simply stating what you are going to do. Try another approach, and you'll be miles ahead.

Provocative or startling statement

Instead of saying "I'm going to explain the new sales compensation program," why not spark their imaginations with a statement like this: "In the next 15 minutes I'm going to explain how each one of you can increase your earnings by 50 percent this year." That's much more likely to get their attention.

Your listeners' reactions to such a statement will be to perk up and be prepared for more information. Now your listeners are participating with you, and you're on the way to establishing understanding.

Statistics

Closely related to the provocative statement—in fact it can be one form of such a statement—is the presentation of a statistic: "Today more than 74 percent of our female employees utilize day-care facilities for their children at a cost of more than $90,000 per year." Or this series of statistics:

The Tax Foundation reports that the average American worked an hour and 27 minutes each day to pay for housing and household operations. Food and beverages take another hour and three minutes. Clothing takes 23 minutes, transportation costs 42 minutes and medical care an average of 30 minutes. But that's only peanuts. The biggest bite of all is taken by federal, state, and local government.

Rhetorical question

A rhetorical question is a thought-provoking question for which you don't expect to get an answer. "Just how much more government interference can our company take?" or "How would you feel if you were turned down for a promotion because of your religious beliefs?"

Sometimes a series of these is effective. "What will we do: when our computers can no longer keep track of customer billing? When claims for refunds cannot be dismissed because we can't get the data we need? When our customers flock to a competitor that offers them bills that are easier to understand? What will we do then?"

Be careful not to overwork this approach. And remember that there is always the danger that some wise guy will *answer* your question and completely deflate your introduction: "How many more people do we have to lose to competition before we wake up?" If someone in the audience deadpans, "11," your intro may fizzle.

Quotation, definition, or short story

Often a short story, quote or light remark can effectively lead into the body of your talk. A talk recommending additional training might build upon a quote from Benjamin Franklin: "If a man empties his purse into his head, no man can take it away from him. If a man invests in learning, he has made the greatest investment." Other examples of quotes and definitions are found at the beginning of each chapter of this book.

Everybody loves to hear a story. So it is no surprise that the short anecdote, especially if it is a personal example, often works beautifully. Simply relate your interesting experiences as though you were telling a friend. Strive for a conversational tone. Don't drag out the story. Use it only as a lead-in to the meat of your talk.

Some people are hesitant about using personal examples. They shouldn't be. Firsthand experiences have vitality and can be explained more clearly than somebody else's stories.

Audience participation

Try using audience participation in your introduction. Asking a few key questions of specific audience members or having the group take a quiz or participate in a simple game may be the best way to get them in tune with your presentation.

"I'd like to ask for your candid remarks about the new building proposals. Martha, what concerns do you have?"

Be sure you don't put people on the spot. Be sensitive to your tone of voice in asking questions. Don't do anything that's likely to embarrass your listeners or make them uncomfortable. Be sure to show your listeners how the questions and answers relate to your theme and purpose.

While on the topic of introductions, let me caution you against some poor approaches that can seriously damage your talk by failing to gain attention, setting an inappropriate theme and destroying your credibility. Avoid:

1. **The apologetic beginning.** Start out by saying something like "Unaccustomed as I am to public speaking, I...," "I'm here to bore you with a few more statistics" or "I'm pretty nervous, so I hope you'll bear with me." If you haven't prepared well enough, it will become obvious soon enough. You accomplish nothing by announcing it.

2. **The potentially offensive beginning.** An off-color joke or ridiculing statement will eventually get you in trouble. You never know for sure how someone will respond to such remarks. Avoid them. You have nothing to gain from their use and much to lose.

3. **Openings that are excessively flattering or just plain phony.** "I am filled with a deep sense of personal inadequacy when I presume to speak authoritatively in the presence of so many knowledgeable men." Ugh!

4. **The gimmicky beginning.** Some people carry creativity a bit too far and come up with gimmicks that fizzle. People who blow whistles, act out scenes from a play, honk horns or write the word *sex* on the blackboard saying "now that I have your attention..." run a serious risk of damaging their credibility. These kinds of things can confuse your listeners or make them feel uncomfortable.

✧ **Action Tip 28** ✧

Use bridges to show how your ideas fit together.

Transition words or phrases provide the links that hold the talk together. They bridge the ideas. Specifically, they typically do the following:

- Briefly recap or summarize what's just been covered.

- Suggest, imply, or state what is to come next.

- Lead into a conclusion.

Good bridge phrases help your listeners shift gears, re-adjust expectations and recap what has been covered. Without transitions it is almost impossible for listeners to follow even a relatively simple line of thought. But you as the speaker also get important advantages from the liberal use of transitions. They give you extra moments to check your notes, change physical position, re-establish eye contact with your audience, check for listener feedback or adjust a visual aid.

Perhaps the simplest way to transition from one topic to the next is to simply announce that you are doing so. For example: "Now that I have explained the history of widget production in the United States, let me now present some exciting new technologies on the horizon of widget-making."

✧ Action Tip 29 ✧

Use action endings to tell listeners what they need to remember.

As you end most presentations you should:

1. Summarize key points.

2. Restate your central theme.

3. Point to the listeners' need to know what you've just told them, and remind them of the urgency (or at least importance) of that information.

4. Provide listeners with a clear action step, a prescribed behavior or mental activity they should *do*.

Summaries are especially useful here to *recap the key ideas* (but not many details) of your talk. Keep in mind how repetition helps us to remember; then use this tool one more time as you lead into your close. Avoid introducing any new material at this point. It may confuse your listeners.

Everything you have done to develop this presentation comes to a climax at the conclusion. So the most important question goes back to your early planning—what was your specific intent? Picture yourself as a listener and ask the tough question: "What does this all mean to me?" Your talk should have provided a clear answer.

Action steps are appropriate for all kinds of presentations. Your listeners have a right to receive guidance from all of your preparation. And if you don't provide such guidance in the form of a clear, action-oriented conclusion, you let them down.

If your presentation is informational (a progress report, for example) and does not call for specific action from your listeners, you may simply want to recap and restate your purpose: "My intention today was to update you regarding the progress of the XYZ project. To summarize, we are on schedule and within budget. If you have specific questions, I am happy to answer them now."

No matter the format or purpose of your presentation, your conclusion need not be elaborate or drawn out. If the rest of the talk is well-done, the conclusion will be self-evident, and you need only restate and bring a sense of finality.

Chapter 8

Get Your Message Across

"Well-timed silence hath more eloquence than speech."

—Martin Farquhar Tupper,
19th-century English
philosopher

This chapter covers two areas of presentation delivery.

- How to create a positive image through our personal delivery style. This is done mostly through our nonverbal messages.

- How to decide what procedures will work best for a given presentation. These procedures include what kinds of notes we should use, how we might use a question-answer session, the amount of listener participation we want, etc.

✦ Action Tip 30 ✦

Deliver your message like a professional.

Anything we do or say (or don't do, or don't say!) can be interpreted by others as having some meaning. Much of our image is projected through nonverbal signals; that is, without words. Although we can't account for all possible interpretations of our nonverbal behaviors, we can become aware of some that most often convey meaning. Several kinds of nonverbal variables are particularly important. Be aware of the potential impact of these:

1. Appearance.

2. Body movement.

3. Facial expression and eye contact.

4. Voice cues and "paralanguage."

Appearance. Dress and grooming should be *appropriate* to the occasion. They should not be so extreme in style that they draw attention away from our message. In other words, your tie or jewelry shouldn't talk louder than you do!

Body movement and gestures. Gestures, posture, and movement can be used to "punctuate" points in your message. On the flip side, they can also be distracting if used inappropriately.

Some people feel uncomfortable using their hands as they speak. For others, it may be said that if you tied their hands they'd be speechless! In my experience, few people overuse gestures—more underuse them. Such movement can go a long way to convey the credibility elements: enthusiasm and dynamism.

Here are several common mistakes people make with gestures:

- They fail to use them where they can be very useful for emphasis.

- They fail to vary them; the same gesture over and over can become monotonous and distracting.

- They use gestures that are too small and cannot be seen clearly. Hand movement should be between the waist and shoulders and out away from the body.

Effective gestures are both purposeful and natural. Nervous gestures such as adjusting your tie, scratching your ear or adjusting your hairdo may feel natural, but they are not purposeful. These can distract your audience or convey that you are ill-at-ease.

For the person who feels uncomfortable using hand gestures, I suggest this: Force yourself to try some. One simple type is to hold up fingers when enumerating key points. ("My third suggestion is...") Continue to experiment with gestures, and make them bigger—more expansive. Your listeners will not sense this exaggeration but will get the impact of your gesture.

Body movement can be very helpful to your presentation. Pausing between key points and moving to another place in the room (it may be only a few inches away) helps your listener know that you have finished one point and will now be shifting to another. This becomes a nonverbal transition or bridge. It helps your listeners follow the organization of your talk.

If you cannot freely move around because you must speak into a microphone, you can still use a pause and a shift in position—even a change in direction where you are looking—to indicate the same thing.

Facial expression and eye contact.

Listeners focus on your face and eyes as you speak. Facial expression almost always conveys how you really feel about what you are saying.

The most important part of the face is the eyes. We expect people to look us in the eyes when they talk to us—not an extended, piercing look, but contact with occasional breaks to blink or look away. People who fail to make sufficient eye contact are perceived as shifty or not to be trusted.

Why do we seek eye contact? Research says that we establish and maintain eye contact when:

- We are seeking feedback or reactions from others.

- We want to signal that we are ready to communicate.

- We want to convey our need for involvement or inclusion in the group to which we are speaking.

Poor eye contact can convey very different messages:

- The speaker wants to hide something.

- There is dislike or tension between people in a communication situation.

- The speaker is telling a lie.

- An individual wants to disavow a social relationship with others.

- The speaker is about to begin a long utterance.

With the exception of the last message listed, the absence of eye contact expresses a desire to avoid communicating.

When talking to a larger group, it is best to look at each person for a few seconds and then move on to others. Don't just scan the crowd—really look at individuals.

Vocal cues

This delivery element is *the way* something is said and not *what* is said. Vocal cues include emphasis and tone of voice that can change the meaning of a message. A man who is obviously enraged (as indicated by his nonverbal cues) and shouts, "I am not angry!" is contradicting the meaning of his words. Another example: A disappointed person who shrugs his shoulders, looks away from his boss and says, "Yeah, that'll be fine."

Examples of potentially distracting vocal cues might be:

- A breathy, whining, or strident voice.

- A bombastic or rapid-fire delivery.

- A dull, expressionless recitation.

Professional communicators are very sensitive to differences in meaning created by emphasis on certain words. When working on our vocal cues, we have several things to focus on. These include articulation, pronunciation, voice quality, and verbalized pauses or filler words. To deliver a presentation like a pro, check how well you are doing at each of these:

Articulation and pronunciation

Some common problems:

- Omitting final consonants (goin instead of going; havin instead of having; ya instead of *you*).

- Omitting sounds (liberry instead of library; tempature instead of temperature; binness instead of business).

- Inserting additional sounds (athalete instead of athlete; "off-ten" instead of often with the t silent).

- Distorted sounds (crick instead of creek, flustrated instead of frustrated).

To avoid such mishaps, it is always helpful to practice your talk carefully. Practice in front of a mirror, ask a friend to listen and critique, or tape your talk and play it back to listen for problems in articulation or pronunciation.

Verbalized pauses or filler words

Few things can irritate your audience as much as the liberal use of "ah," "um," "uh" and the ever popular, "you know." Tape yourself, and count the number of filler words you use.

Voice variation

Beware of the monotone. Change your voice pitch liberally. Allow some energy and emotion into your voice. Emphasize important points by raising your voice—or speaking very softly so that the audience listens more intently.

Some speakers do not want to "risk" much variation. They fear sounding silly. But failing to vary pitch is throwing away one of your most useful tools. Listen carefully to successful radio or TV announcers, whose behaviors exemplify good delivery style.

✧ Action Tip 31 ✧

Avoid overuse of notes.

A formal manuscript—that is, a word-for-word copy of the talk—is seldom used in oral presentations. The only advantage of a manuscript is that it allows for precise expression and a written record of what exactly was said. This can be important in diplomacy and some formal negotiations. The drawback, of course, is that the speaker *sounds* as if he is reading to us.

For most presentations, it makes more sense to prepare your presentation well and use a few notes or an outline to guide you. The amount of detail in your notes will vary, but this more informal way of speaking always permits more flexibility. You can more easily adjust to your audience.

How much should you put in your notes? My advice is, when in doubt, leave it out. More speakers err on the side of too many notes than too few. Detailed notes become a security blanket. The more you have written, the more you are likely to look it them. The danger in having such notes is, of course, that you lose eye contact with your listeners.

Many speakers prefer to use note cards rather than sheets of paper. They're less distracting. Others have found that good visual aids can almost take the place of notes.

Some speakers use pictures or sketches to jog the memory. The pictures work because the brain can translate pictures faster that it can read and assimilate words. Also, because there are no words to read, the speaker is forced to put the idea into his or her own language, resulting in a more natural, conversational tone.

Remember, your notes or pictures don't have to be recognizable to anyone but you.

Regardless of whether you use notes, pictures, visual aids, or a manuscript, it is *crucial that you practice the presentation out loud* before actually delivering it. There is no substitute for this. Period.

Chapter 9

Give Them Something to Look At

"I hear and I forget. I see and I remember. I do and I understand."

—Chinese proverb

Virtually anyone you speak to today is a product of the TV generation. We are not accustomed to processing spoken words alone—we need to *see* something, too. Studies of listener comprehension repeatedly come to the same conclusion: *Visual aids help listeners get and remember the message.*

As helpful as visuals are to your listeners, they can also help you in *delivery* by providing an outline of key thoughts, increasing your self-confidence, permitting natural action and movement, and diverting attention away from the speaker and toward the message. The overall result is an improved audience impression of you as a speaker.

✧ Action Tip 32 ✧

Visuals help the listeners *and* you.

Visual aids serve at least four important functions:

1. They help clarify abstract or confusing ideas in the minds of listeners.

2. They help listeners retain information—illustrated ideas linger in the mind.

3. They help fight the speaker's enemies: listener boredom, daydreaming, confusion, and apathy.

4. They serve as guides to keep the speaker on track—they can replace notes.

The single most important point to remember about visuals is to keep them *simple and concise*. Simple design lingers in the mind of the receiver best.

Here are some simple types of direct visuals and suggestions as to how to make them.

Word chart posters

A word chart is probably your simplest visual. As its name implies, this is simply text displayed on a poster. In preparing word charts, economy of language is crucial—use short, clear words. Be sure that the lettering is large so that everyone in your audience can read it.

Sample word chart

```
PURPOSES OF PERFORMANCE
         APPRAISAL:

1.  Provides data for promotions,
    transfers, terminations, etc.

2.  Identifies training needs

3.  Provides feedback to employees

4.  Provides basis for reward allocation
```

Flip charts

These are large tablets of paper mounted on an easel. They are inexpensive and can be adapted to a variety of situations. You can prepare them in advance and add to them during the presentation, or start out with blank sheets and have your listeners mentally participate with you as you write or draw. They are also good for recording ideas shared by your listeners. Flip charts are usually used in informal presentations and work best with small to medium-sized groups, say 20 or fewer people.

A trick: You can put notes in light pencil on the flip chart to remind you of what to write.

Pie charts, line graphs, and bar or column charts

A pie chart is a simple, circular illustration that is divided into segments to show part-to-whole comparisons. It can effectively show only a few broad divisions. A line graph gives a continuous picture showing trends or changes over time as shown below. It can also show simple comparisons or trends when showing several lines. Avoid having too many lines on the chart—it gets too confusing. Color coding can be helpful to clarify the message. The bar or column chart can quickly compare quantities. The bar chart uses a horizontal design; column charts are vertical. Other than that, they are the same.

The types of charts and graphs described above can be easily produced using presentation software such as PowerPoint™, Corel Presentations™ and Harvard Graphics.™ Typically, with such programs, you simply tell the computer the numbers or percentages and the type of graphic you want, and it does the rest.

Sample line chart

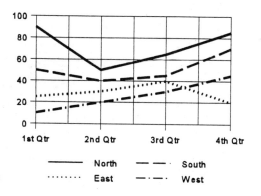

Sample column chart

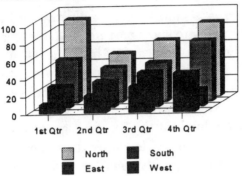

Sample bar chart

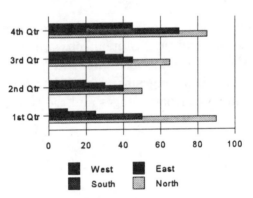

Props, models, or samples

When your audience is small, you may want to use props, models, or samples to show exactly what you are talking about. If you are talking about selling shoes, you would probably want to use sample shoes to convince your audience.

When giving a talk to explain the workings of a new machine, it obviously makes sense to have the machine there as a prop if possible.

Projected visuals

Projected visuals (these include overhead transparencies and slides) have two major advantages over direct visuals.

1. They are less cumbersome to use.

2. They can project a larger image to audiences who may not be able to see direct visuals.

The simplest projected visual to use is the overhead transparency. Today's transparency projectors are portable, quiet, and capable of reproducing a sharp image. The transparencies themselves can be made very simply, often using a photocopy as a master.

This ease of use can also be a drawback to transparencies: They are so easy to make that people copy anything without thinking about how clearly it will project. Never make a transparency from a page of text; it's too complicated. Also, be sure drawings are large enough. If too small, enlarge them on a photocopier before you make a transparency.

Felt-tip pens designed for writing on transparencies permit the speaker to add his or her own handwriting to a transparency on display. In situations where a chalkboard or flip chart is not available, presenters can simply write on a blank transparency sheet as they speak. This would be projected on a wall or screen for easy viewing by the audience. This has the added benefit of allowing the speaker to maintain eye contact, continuing to face the audience as he or she writes on the transparency.

The most common mistake in using transparencies is putting too much information on each page. Keep them simple.

An added touch is to mount transparencies on frames or in transparent sleeves. The sleeves provide a fold-out frame as well as a three-hole margin to keep transparencies in a notebook. This adds professionalism and keeps the transparencies from sticking together or sliding due to static electricity buildup. Another advantage: The frames provide a good place to write your notes and key ideas. Such frames can be purchased at office supply stores.

Slides

Photographic slides can be excellent visuals. Three sources of good slides are: 1) custom shot slides using a 35mm or digital camera; 2) photographic slides purchased or shot-to-order by a professional photographer; or 3) computer programs such as those described earlier for making transparencies.

Making the best of visuals

When designing and using direct or projected visuals, remember these key rules:

1. Keep them *simple.*

2. Keep them *clear.* (Use different colors, shadings, or line sizes to highlight key information.)

3. Place or project the visual where it can be seen by everyone. (Don't stand in front of it as you explain the material.)

4. Don't talk to the visual aid; maintain eye contact with your listeners.

5. Display the visual only when it is in use. (Showing it too early or, in some cases, leaving it up too long, can be distracting.)

6. Be sure the visual is large enough to be seen by all listeners. If you have to say, "I know you can't read this, but...," don't use it.

7. Use visuals to support your credibility as well as important ideas in your presentation. (The time and effort of creating visuals conveys to your audience that your talk is important.)

Dynamic visuals

A dynamic visual is one that can show motion and sound. The most common types are movies and video tapes. Traditionally the cost of producing dynamic visuals has been high, but that is changing rapidly.

Quality videotapes can be produced almost as easily as an audiotape recording. Video cassettes are easy to store and play back, and the cost of equipment is very reasonable.

Dynamic visuals can be especially useful in showing people's behaviors in training situations. Teachers have helped students make major progress using videotapes in communication workshops. Participants in role-play situations ranging from presentational speaking to interviews, from meeting management to performance appraisals, can benefit from an objective view of themselves in action provided by videotaping. It can be a real eye-opener.

Positioning your listeners and visuals

To get ideas across and encourage participation, be aware of options in seating. Don't feel locked in to "theater style" rows of seats or even a conference table. Move the furniture around!

Check out the presentation room and the equipment you'll need in advance. Arrive early enough to test equipment. Bring spare projector bulbs. Check out the videotape player or slide projector. Make sure your tape or slide tray is cued up to the right place before you begin. Don't rewind or advance a tape while your audience waits. Know your equipment, and use it smoothly.

A Closing
Thought

As suggested at the beginning of this book, I recommend that you go back to the self-evaluation in Action Tip 1 and retake the "quiz." See what you've learned from this brief book. Then apply all that you now know, and make those truly *winning* presentations!

Because we live in an increasingly complex world, the ability to share ideas with others becomes essential to personal and professional success. Our ability to communicate effectively using the kinds of ideas presented in this brief book can and will determine the kinds of relationships we will have with others.

Today more than ever, we can confidently repeat Lee Iacocca's quote that appeared at the beginning of this book. Communication really *is* the most important thing we can learn—in school, in the world of business, or in our personal lives. The skills needed for winning presentations are the success skills for life.

About the Author

Dr. Paul R. Timm is best known for bringing powerful, practical ideas to thousands of people through his writing, teaching, video programs, and speaking. He has served as consultant and trainer to numerous corporations, associations, and government agencies, dealing with challenges and opportunities in customer service, human relations, personal effectiveness, and communication.

Timm has nearly 30 years of front-line experience in people management, motivation, and business skill-building. He has held leadership positions with Xerox Corporation, Martin Marietta, Bell South, and was president of a training firm, Prime Learning International. He has continued to research contemporary management challenges, having received research grants from JCPenney Corporation and others. He serves on the editorial advisory board for Dartnell Corporation and Parke-Davis Pharmaceutical's *Patient Service Initiative* publications. His consulting focuses on customer service and retention in retail, financial, and health care organizations.

An active author, Timm has written 31 books and dozens of articles. He also wrote and appears in six videotape training programs produced by JWA Video of Chicago.

He earned university degrees from the State University of New York at Buffalo (bachelor's degree), Ohio University (master's degree), and Florida State University (Ph.D.) Dr. Timm has taught at three major universities and currently serves as chair of the Organizational Leadership and Strategy Department at the Marriott School of Management, Brigham Young University.

Index

Winning Telephone Tips,
How to Hold Successful Meetings
and
How to Make Winning Presentations
by Dr. Paul R. Timm

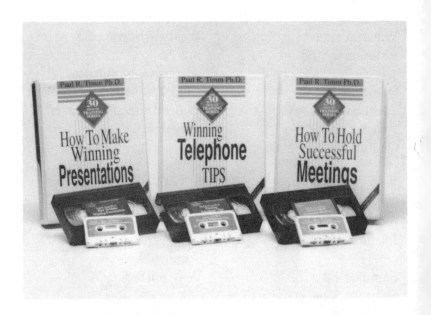

Winning Telephone Tips,
How to Hold Successful Meetings
and
How to Make Winning Presentations
by Dr. Paul R. Timm

Improve your telephone skills and increase your profits! You'll learn why it's important to ace your own telephone calls, how to avoid unnecessary call screening and how to make ur voice-mail more efficient with **Winning Telephone Tips.**

Are meetings a valuable business tool or a waste of time? When should a meeting be held d when should a meeting be avoided? Learn to make meetings work for you with **How to ld Successful Meetings.**

Take the mystery and fear out of making a speech or a presentation with **How to Make inning Presentations.** Learn to feel comfortable and in control when speaking before one 1,000 people.

Each training program comes with a videocassette, audiocassette and copy of the book for ty $99.95.

st call toll-free, 1-800-327-5110.
u may use MasterCard, Visa or American Express.

complete the order form below and mail to the address in the aded area.

✂ cut here ✂

JWA/Video, 921 W. VanBuren St., Suite 220, Chicago, IL 60607

Send me ____ copy(ies) of *Winning Telephone Tips.* ($99.95)

Send me ____ copy(ies) of *How to Hold Successful Meetings.* ($99.95)

Send me ____ copy(ies) of *How to Make Winning Presentations.* ($99.95)

me _____

dress _____

y _____ State _____ Zip _____

y Phone _____ Evening Phone _____

Enclosed is a check for $_____.   ❏ PO #_____

Please charge $_____ to my credit card.* ❏ Visa   ❏ MasterCard

_____

redit card number)   (Exp. date)   (Signature)